Queens of the Ice

Queens of the Ice

*They were fast, they were fierce,
they were teenage girls*

Carly Adams

James Lorimer & Company Ltd., Publishers
Toronto

James Lorimer & Company Ltd., Publishers acknowledges the support of the Ontario Arts Council. We acknowledge the financial support of the Government of Canada through the Canada Book Fund for our publishing activities. We acknowledge the support of the Canada Council for the Arts for our publishing program. We acknowledge the Government of Ontario through the Ontario Media Development Corporation's Ontario Book Initiative.

Cover design: Meredith Bangay

Library and Archives Canada Cataloguing in Publication

Adams, Carly
        Queens of the ice : they were fast, they were fierce, they were teenage girls / Carly Adams.

Includes index.
Also issued in electronic format.
ISBN 978-1-55277-721-3 (bound).—ISBN 978-1-55277-720-6 (pbk.)

        1. Preston Rivulettes (Hockey team)–History. 2. Hockey for women–Ontario–Cambridge–History. I. Title.

GV848.6.W65A33 2011   796.962082'0971345   C2011-900220-5

James Lorimer & Company Ltd., Publishers
317 Adelaide Street West,
Suite #1002
Toronto, ON, Canada
M5V 1P9
www.lorimer.ca

Distributed in the
United States by:
Orca Book Publishers
P.O. Box 468
Custer, WA USA
98240-0468

Printed and bound in Canada.
Manufactured by Webcom in Toronto,
Ontario, Canada in February, 2011.
Job # 375121

MIX
Paper from
responsible sources
FSC® C004071

This book is dedicated to all of the players of the Preston Rivulettes. These women were phenomenal hockey players who have left a legacy that should not be forgotten.

This book is also for Jay and Quinn.

Contents

Prologue

It's a cold winter day in February 1931. Under the wooden roof of the arena, the players from Preston and the visiting team from Grimsby skate to their places on the ice. One puck and two teams, each with five players and a goalie. It is the semifinals of the Ontario championships and both teams want to win.

The game begins at centre ice. The two centre players lean forward, ready to leap on the puck. The ref drops it and they're off.

Preston's Ranscombe wins the faceoff. Ranscombe carries the puck down the ice and slides a pass to Schmuck in the left wing. The home team dominates the play. Shot after shot, they pepper the Grimsby goalie with pucks. It's a fast game with lots of offence. Webb follows in fast after a shot from Schmuck bounces off the crossbar and flicks the disc into the net. Three minutes later Ranscombe races down the ice, pushing through the opposing team. The goalie is shocked as the puck sails into the top of the net. During the first period, the Grimsby team doesn't get a single shot on net.

The second period is tense. The fans sitting on wooden benches are on the edge of their seats. On the ice, both teams have to keep the other team out of their zone and defend the net. The visitors come out hard and are able to reach the net. In the first minute of play, the visitors surprise the home team and slip the puck past the goalie into the net. But the home team is still ahead 2–1.

In the third period, the visitors can't keep up their defences against the mighty home team. Ranscombe slips around the back of the net to outwit the visitors' goalie and scores the home team's third goal. Minutes later Webb receives a pass from Schmuck and shoots the puck hard into the net, securing the game. The referee hands out six penalties: four to Preston for rough play and high-sticking, and two to Grimsby for similar offences.

The Preston Rivulettes win the game 4–1. They play hockey that shows seasons of practise. The fans in the stands are surprised by the game. Most people had not expected women to be so good at hockey!

1 Girls Want to Play

The Preston Rivulettes were the most successful women's hockey team in history. They played together for ten seasons, from 1931 until 1940. They had an amazing record. They played about a hundred games and lost only two of them!

The story of the Preston Rivulettes begins with one player: Hilda Ranscombe. Hilda was the youngest of nine children. She was born in 1917, in Preston, Ontario. Preston was a small town about

Hilda Ranscombe

100 kilometres (62 miles) southwest of Toronto. Today it is a part of the city of Cambridge.

Hilda loved to play hockey. Every chance she got, she grabbed her stick and ran down to the Grand or Speed River. After stopping behind Clare's foundry to tie on her skates, she met with other boys

The Preston Rivulettes softball team

and girls from town to play. When there was no one to play against, Hilda went to a pond near her home by the Rocks Springs Brewery. There she skated for hours and hours. She practised handling and shooting the puck. Long hours of practise made Hilda a fast skater and a hard shooter, and she was determined to be the best.

Thirteen-year-old Hilda and her older sister Nellie loved to play all kinds of sports. They played on a softball team during the summer called the Preston Rivulettes. But when the softball season ended and winter came, there were no team sports for girls and women in their town.

At the end of the 1930 baseball season, the girls decided they wanted a sport to play during the long winter months. Like Hilda, all of the girls grew up skating on local rivers and ponds, playing pickup games with neighbourhood kids. They decided that they wanted to play on a girls' hockey team. But there was a problem. There wasn't a hockey team for girls in Preston.

So they decided to start one!

One day, a man at the ball diamond overheard the girls talking about their plans. He bet them that they would not be able to do this. He didn't think girls could play hockey. This gave the girls even more reason to find a way to play. But how exactly would they start a hockey team?

The girls heard that sportswriter Alexandrine Gibb was staying in town

The Preston Rivulettes softball team

at the Kress House Hotel. They loved to read her column, "No Man's Land of Sport" in the *Toronto Daily Star* newspaper. They were nervous about talking to one of Canada's top women sports journalists. But they wanted to get her advice.

Alexandrine was glad to hear their idea to start a girls hockey team. She explained that there were teams in other towns that were part of a league with the Ladies Ontario Hockey Association. She told them to join the league. She also suggested

Female Sports Reporters

Beginning in the 1920s, major Canadian newspapers hired women to write newspaper columns about women's sports. These columns were important sources of information for players and fans. The female sports reporters told women how they could get involved in organizing or playing on teams. They also offered their opinions about how sports should be played. Some of the most influential women sportswriters in Canada around this time were:

- Myrtle Cook, who wrote "In the Women's Sportlight" for the *Montreal Daily Star*, 1929–1970s
- Alexandrine Gibb, who wrote "No Man's Land of Sport" for the *Toronto Daily Star*, 1928–1940
- Phyllis Griffiths, who wrote "The Girl and the Game" for the *Toronto Telegram*, 1928–1942
- Bobbie Rosenfeld, who wrote "Feminine Sports Reel" for the Toronto *Globe and Mail*, 1937–1958
- Patricia Page Hollingsworth, who wrote "Feminine Flashes" for the *Edmonton Journal*, 1935–1940

that they should get the support of a town businessman.

Hilda and her teammates took Alexandrine's advice. They went to see Karl Homuth, their local Member of Parliament. He helped them find a coach and provided them with the money they needed to get started.

At the first Rivulettes team practice, ten players stepped onto the ice: Nellie Ranscombe (Hilda's sister) as goalie; Grace Webb and Margaret Gabbitas to play defence; sisters Helen and Marm Schmuck as forwards with Hilda Ranscombe; and Myrtle Parr, Pat Marriot, and two others as alternates. All of the players were teenagers between the ages of 13 and 19. Herb Fach, the manager of the Lowther Street arena, agreed to coach the team. He was ready to get the team in shape for the season.

Ice Time for Girls

The Rivulettes had trouble finding enough ice time to practise and play games. This was surprising since their coach was the manager of the local arena. But the boys and men's teams had first choice of ice times. This is still often a challenge for girls and women playing hockey today, especially in small towns and cities where there are only one or two indoor arenas.

All of the Rivulettes were in high school or worked full-time. Nellie Ranscombe and Marm and Helen Schmuck worked at the Wragge Shoe Company and the Savage Shoe Company. Myrtle Parr worked as a secretary at the Bank of Montreal. Hilda Ranscombe had graduated from high school and lived at home with her mother. She helped with household chores and taking care of her younger brothers and sisters.

Because of the players' work and school commitments, the evening was the best time to practise. But this was also the hardest time to find ice. The team often had to practise at odd times. But they made it work. They wanted to be a great hockey team.

2 They Shoot! They Score!

By the time the Rivulettes stepped onto the ice in the 1930s, girls and women had been playing hockey for a long time. In fact, girls and women have played hockey in Canada for over one hundred years, since the 1880s!

The house of Lord and Lady Stanley in Ottawa is known as the place of the first women's hockey game. Lord Stanley was Canada's sixth Governor General. When the Stanleys arrived in Ottawa in 1888

The Stanley Cup

Lord Stanley is best remembered for donating the Stanley Cup to men's hockey. In 1892, the cup was given as the trophy for Canada's best amateur hockey team. Since 1926, it has been the championship trophy for the National Hockey League.

from London, England, they went to the Winter Carnival in Montreal. There, they watched a hockey match between the Montreal Vics and the Montreal Amateur Athletic Association.

Lord Stanley fell in love with hockey. He went back to Ottawa, found a pair of skates and a stick, and tried the sport. He encouraged his family to play, too. His eight sons and two daughters all played together on a pond near their home. The Stanleys often hosted skating parties. At these parties pickup hockey games, with men and women, were often played. Lord Stanley's daughter, Isobel, loved the sport too. She became one of the first female hockey players in Canada. She played for a Government House team. Many other women also wanted to join in the fun after reading about games in the local newspaper.

Early women's hockey was a social affair. Women got together to talk, catch up on news, and spend time with friends. In 1902, a match between the ladies' hockey clubs of Trois-Rivières and Montreal was called the "Championship of Canada."

Over the years, the social matches changed into more organized leagues, games, and tournaments. By the beginning of World War I in 1914, there were teams in many small towns and bigger cities across Canada. There were teams in the Maritimes, Ontario, Quebec, British Columbia, and even as far north as the

Raising Money for War

During World War I and World War II, women formed groups to provide clothing to soldiers and raise money for the war effort. Sports were one way women could raise money. Hockey and softball teams staged exhibition games with the proceeds going towards the war.

Yukon. The teams played mostly outdoors on ponds and frozen rivers. Indoor ice was rare at this time. Girls and women often played hockey matches to raise money for charity or to help send Canadian soldiers off to war.

Back in the early 1900s, a lot of people did not think girls should play hockey. They thought girls lacked the strength to play competitive sports. Others worried that girls would hurt themselves. Even some doctors thought that if women played physical sports like hockey, they would damage their bodies and would not be able to have children. Many girls and women disagreed with these beliefs. They loved hockey and they wanted to play!

In 1922, the Ladies Ontario Hockey Association (LOHA) formed. It was the first governing body for women's hockey in Ontario. The LOHA organized leagues across Ontario. There were teams from as far east as Ottawa and as far west as St. Thomas, with many of the teams from Toronto. The LOHA patterned itself on the men's Ontario Hockey Association but they were a separate organization. They ran women's hockey in the province until 1940.

3 The First Season

For the Preston Rivulettes' first season, Coach Fach arranged for them to enter the intermediate league of the LOHA. This was a league for new teams. The team hoped it would soon get to play in the senior league with the best teams in the province. They entered the season late in January 1931, so they had to play a qualifying match against the Grimsby Peaches to earn a spot in the playoffs. They wore bright red and white jerseys

Ticket Prices

Tickets to Rivulettes games cost 25 cents for adults and 15 cents for children. In 1930, 25 cents was a lot of money. It could buy three boxes of cereal or four cans of soup.

with a giant P on the front for Preston.

During the two-game series against Grimsby, the Rivulettes played fast and aggressive hockey. Their smooth stickhandling impressed the crowd. Most of the time, they kept the puck in the Peaches' end. Shot after shot, the Rivulettes offence bombarded the Grimsby goalie. Fifteen minutes into the first game, forward Grace Webb scored the Rivulettes' first goal on a pass from Marm Schmuck. Three minutes later Hilda Ranscombe scored on a breakaway. The Rivulettes won the first game 4–1 and the second 5–1 for a combined series score of 9–2.

LADIES HOCKEY
Semi-Final Game
PORT DOVER
1929-1930 Champions, &c.
PRESTON RIVULETTES
AT PRESTON ARENA
Tonight, Thur., Feb. 26th, 8.30
Added Attraction at 9.30
Hespeler Church League Play-off
Admission 25c.   Children 15c.

Next up — the Port Dover Sailorettes
in the quarter-finals. The Sailorettes were
the 1929 and 1930 Ontario champions.
The first game of the quarter-finals was
played in Preston. The Sailorettes were
a good team with skilful players. They
also had a lot of players. With a bigger
team, each player did not have to play
the whole game. When players were tired
they could catch their breath at the side of
the ice before returning to the game. The
Rivulettes had a small team and all of the
players often played the whole 60-minute

game without a break. But in the end, the Sailorettes were no match for the mighty Rivulettes. They failed to match the speed and skill of the locals. With Hilda Ranscombe scoring the only goal, the Rivulettes won the first game 1–0.

Many Preston fans travelled to Port Dover for the second game to cheer on the Rivulettes. The Rivulettes attracted a lot of fans. The people in the town loved supporting a winning team. The Rivulettes didn't let them down. After a hard-fought game, they pulled out another close victory with a score of 1–0.

The Rivulettes were such skilful hockey players that some people thought they must be boys disguised as girls. In fact, the Port Dover coach wanted Helen Schmuck to take off her clothes to prove she was a girl!

The Rivulettes met the London Silverwoods in the semifinals. The first

Chaperones

Several older women acted as chaperones for the Rivulettes when they travelled to other towns. In the 1930s, many people believed that girls and young women needed to be watched to make sure they did not get into trouble. It was not proper for teenage girls and unmarried women to be alone with men. Often it was the wives of the coaches or managers who chaperoned the team.

game of the series took place on home ice in Preston. The arena was packed with 942 cheering fans. The weather was mild and the natural ice in the arena was soft. This made it hard to skate. But the Rivulettes kept forcing the play throughout the game. The Schmuck sisters and Hilda Ranscombe were the Rivulettes' best forward line. They played the entire game and kept up the pressure on the visitors net. Their backchecking kept the London team away from the Rivulettes' net.

It was a rough game with lots of hits and many penalties handed out by the ref. In the second period, Rivulettes forward Helen Schmuck was hit on the side of the mouth by a flying puck. The cut drew blood but she did not go off the ice. The crowd clapped and cheered when she decided to keep playing. After 60 minutes of play, the Rivulettes defeated London 2–0.

The second game was also a battle. The Rivulettes managed to end the game with a 1–0 win. Their winning streak was still intact. They had not lost a game all season!

The Ontario finals for the intermediate league took place in the middle of March in Belleville. Only one game was played to determine the winner between the Rivulettes and the Pembroke Ladies. This was the first time that either team played in a provincial hockey final.

When the Rivulettes arrived in

Knockout!

In the 1920s and early 1930s, women's hockey was fast and hard-hitting with bodychecking and lots of penalties. Newspaper reports are filled with stories of fights and rough play. Some newspaper headlines read: "Sticks and Fists Fly Freely as Girl Hockeyists Battle," "Girls Wanted Another Fight But Referees Stopped Them," "Hockey Amazons in Fistic Display." Many people, including news reporters, criticized women for playing like men. The LOHA changed the rules in 1936, removing bodychecking from the women's game in Ontario. However, this had little impact on the game — women still played hockey with hard hits and fighting on the ice.

Belleville, they were escorted through town to the arena by a parade of cars and a marching band. Back home, fans in Preston waited by their radios to hear the play-by-play broadcast of the game on the local radio station.

The Preston Rivulettes vs. . .

Some of the teams the Rivulettes played against in the 1930s were:

- the Brantford YWCA
- the Port Dover Sailorettes
- the London Silverwoods
- the Grimsby Peaches
- the Ottawa Rangers
- the Guelph Leaflettes
- the Kitchener Freddie-Jacks
- the Kitchener Wentworths
- the Toronto Pats
- the Hamilton Moodie Tigers
- the Stratford Aces
- the Toronto Ladies
- the Pembroke Ladies

The Rivulettes forward line of Hilda Ranscombe and Marm and Helen Schmuck dominated the play. In attack after attack they swept through the front line of the Pembroke team, forcing the

The Preston Rivulettes in 1932

goalie to make desperate saves and defend her net as best she could. The Pembroke girls were heavier and older with more experience, but they could not keep up with the fast skating Rivulettes. In every period of the game the Rivulettes proved they were the better team. After fighting hard for three periods, the Rivulettes won the game 4–2.

They were Ontario champs at the intermediate level.

When the team returned to Preston, friends, family, and fans lined King Street to greet them. People waited hours in the cold for them to come home. The town band played for them. The Rivulettes were Ontario champs and their victory called for a huge town celebration.

4 Moving Up

It looked like the Rivulettes could not be beat. They were good and they knew it. After winning the 1931 intermediate championship, they challenged the Toronto Silverwoods, the senior division champs, to a match. It was a benefit game to raise money for Rivulettes goalie Helen Schmuck, who was confined to her home with an illness.

It was an exciting game in front of 1,475 spectators. Both teams were fast.

Sick From Playing Hockey?

The local newspaper reported that Rivulettes goalie Helen Schmuck was sick because of playing hockey. They wrote: "Helen Schmuck whose sensational playing had everything to do with the team's fine achievement and who through her unsparing efforts so lowered her vitality and resistance that she suffered a breakdown." Women on teams had to always prove that they were just as able to play hockey as boys and men.

Forward lines controlled and passed the puck with skill. Defence players fiercely protected their net from attackers. At the end of three periods of intense play, with hard hits and strong backchecking, the Rivulettes and the Silverwoods were tied 2–2. The sudden-death overtime period had fans on the edge of their seats. Five minutes into the period, Hilda accepted a pass from Marm and fired the puck over the left shoulder of the goalie. The Rivulettes won 3–2. After only a few months on the ice, they could play hockey with the best teams in Ontario.

Despite the win against Toronto, the senior champions, the Rivulettes remained in the intermediate division for the 1932 season. They were disappointed that they were not asked to move up to the senior division, but they knew if they kept winning they would be asked in time.

Their league for the 1932 season was made up of three teams: the Rivulettes, the Guelph Leaflettes and the Kitchener Wentworths. The Guelph and Kitchener teams were no match for the Rivulettes, who won all of their league and playoff games.

They were so good that they were starting to wonder if they could be the best team in Canada!

The Rivulettes met Chalk River in the

Natural Ice

Most hockey arenas in the 1930s had natural ice surfaces, not artificial ice. This meant the quality of the ice depended on the weather. If the temperature outside was too warm, the ice could turn to slush. Sometimes games had to be postponed until the temperature dropped.

Ontario finals. Every player on the team was in top form and turned in a great effort on the ice. The Rivulettes took the offensive from the drop of the puck. They pushed Chalk River back into their own end time and time again. But it was left-winger Marm Schmuck who led the team to victory. In the opening period she scored two goals, taking the lead for her team. In the second period Hilda Ranscombe stickhandled her way through the opposing team to score the final goal.

It was a 3–0 win for the Rivulettes, and their second Ontario title.

In 1933, it was a similar story. The Rivulettes played against the Guelph Leaflettes, the Kitchener Freddie-Jacks, and the London Silverwoods. They won every league and playoff game they played. There was only one division that year — the senior division. There were not enough teams for two divisions. There were two reasons for the decrease in the number of teams: it was a mild winter and it was the height of the Depression.

Because of the warmer temperatures, the ice was poor for much of the season. By the third period of many games the ice was covered with slush, making it difficult to skate or move the puck.

The Great Depression made it difficult for teams to play hockey. Many teams did not have enough money to travel to other towns and cities for games.

The Great Depression

The Great Depression began in 1929 with a stock market crash in the United States. The poor economy quickly spread to Canada and the rest of the world. World trade plunged and incomes dropped. Rural areas suffered as crop prices lowered. The longest and most widespread depression of the 20th century, the Great Depression lasted ten years.

In the semifinal round of the Ontario playoffs, the Rivulettes met their rivals — the Port Dover Sailorettes. The first game was a resounding victory for the Rivulettes, with a score of 3–0. But it was also the first game of the year that Hilda Ranscombe did not score.

In front of 400 fans, the Rivulettes tied the Sailorettes 2–2 in the second game of the series. It was a rough game, with tempers flaring. Ten penalties were handed out: six to the Rivulettes and four to the Sailorettes.

The *Galt Daily Reporter* wrote: "Rough, in comparison with previous games, the fans were given a flash of maidenly temper at intervals while the players used their sticks rather freely." That was the first game the Rivulettes had tied since they began playing as a team. But with the series score 5–2, their undefeated record was still intact.

The Rivulettes played the Toronto Ladies in the Ontario finals. In the 1930s, Toronto had several women's hockey teams. They were a much bigger city and there were a larger number of players to draw from. Because of this, Toronto teams often had stronger players than teams from smaller towns. Teams from Toronto also had more money because there were more people to support them.

The winner of the Toronto versus

The Fanny Rosenfeld Trophy

In 1949, Fanny "Bobbie" Rosenfeld was named the top Canadian female athlete of the first half-century. She was a star in many sports, including basketball, softball, tennis, and golf. In 1928, at the Olympics in Amsterdam, she won a gold and a silver medal in Track and Field. Hockey was her real passion. She was one of the best players in Ontario. In the early 1930s, she donated a trophy for the Senior Provincial Women's Hockey Championship.

Preston match would receive the Fanny Rosenfeld Trophy.

The game came to sudden death and the Rivulettes and the Toronto team battled for the prize. On the ice for the Toronto team was Fanny "Bobbie" Rosenfeld herself. In the end the Rivulettes beat the Toronto team, winning their third Ontario title in a row and taking home the trophy.

5 Going National

For the 1933 season, the Rivulettes were heading into new territory.

After winning the Ontario title, they were chosen to represent Eastern Canada in the first ever national finals for women's hockey.

The Dominion Women's Amateur Hockey Association (DWAHA) was formed in 1933. Its goal was to establish a yearly national championship for women's hockey.

The Western champs were the Edmonton Rustlers. The Edmonton team was formed in 1929. The Rustlers, like the Rivulettes, had been provincial champs every year they had been playing.

The Rustlers hosted the National Championship, so the Rivulettes had to travel to Edmonton. For most of the players, it was their first trip out of Ontario. At 9:05 p.m. on Wednesday, March 15, the Rivulettes boarded a train heading west. Two hundred fans filled the platform at the train station to wish the team luck and see them off. Hazel Ruttier, president of the LOHA, was there. Connie Henessy, president of the Toronto Ladies Athletic Club, presented the Rivulettes with a box of chocolates for their trip on behalf of the Toronto Ladies team.

After a three-day train journey, the Rivulettes arrived in Edmonton. Their first game against the Rustlers was just

The Edmonton Rustlers

five short hours after they arrived. Back in Preston, the game was broadcast on the local CKPC radio station.

The Rivulettes stepped onto the ice at the Edmonton arena in front of over 2,000 spectators. Clarence Campbell, future NHL president, refereed the games. In the first period Eleanore Tufford and Muriel Duncan scored for the Rustlers, taking an early two-goal lead. The Rivulettes were

Full House

Compared to women's hockey today, games in the early 1930s attracted a lot of attention. It was common for over 2,000 spectators to crowd into arenas to watch matches. Provincial and National Championships were especially popular.

shocked. They had never been down at the beginning of a game.

The Rivulettes regrouped for the second period. With some fast skating and careful stickhandling, Hilda Ranscombe and Marm Schmuck managed to outwit the Rustlers' goalie twice. The game was tied. But the Rivulettes were tired from their journey. They could not keep up with the Rustlers in the third period. A Rustlers forward broke through the defence and scored. The game was over. The Rivulettes lost 3–2.

It was the first loss for the Rivulettes in three years. Their undefeated record was broken.

It was more bad news for the Rivulettes in the second game of the series. Not able to recover, the Rivulettes suffered a second loss to the Rustlers at 1–0 for a series score of 4–2.

The Edmonton Rustlers were the first National Champions of women's hockey in Canada.

The Rivulettes lost the series, but they were still heroes in Preston. When they returned to Ontario, they were met at the train station by their fans, friends, and families. A parade and a town banquet were held to honour them and celebrate their achievement. By competing for the Canadian title they had put the small town of Preston on the map.

After the defeat in Edmonton, the Rivulettes decided they would continue

The Preston Rivulettes in Edmonton,
Alberta, in March 1933

to practise and work hard to be the best.
They wanted to be national champs.

The Rivulettes had a great season in
1934. They won all of their league games
easily.

At the beginning of March, they met the
Toronto Vagabonds in a two-game series
for the Ontario title. The Rivulettes and
the Vagabonds were both skilled teams

with a lot of talented players. At first it looked like it would be another easy victory for the Rivulettes. Within three minutes of play the Schmuck-Ranscombe-Schmuck forward line grabbed the puck and attacked the net, scoring two quick goals. But Toronto stepped up their defence and unleashed strong plays into Preston's end. Halfway through the first period, a Toronto forward dumped the puck into the net to make the score 2–1. At the 1:30 mark of the second period, the Toronto left-winger rushed the puck into the net to tie the game 2–2. The Rivulettes fought back. Helen Schmuck grabbed the puck at the end of the second period and flipped it in over the goalie's head to score. The Rivulettes pulled out a close 3–2 win.

The newspaper declared the second game the "best game of the season" for the Rivulettes. The forward line led attack after attack on the Toronto net. The *Galt Reporter* wrote:

"The prettiest play of the evening was dished up by Hilda Ranscombe who took the puck from behind her own net to travel the length of the ice to score. She outskated the entire Toronto team and stick-handled her way right in on top of the Toronto goalie and flipped the puck over her head. She received a big hand from the crowd."

With a 3–1 win in the second game and a 6–3 score for the series, the Rivulettes were Ontario champs for the fourth time.

Next up — the Montreal Maroons in the first ever Eastern Canadian Championship. Preston was invited to Montreal for one sudden-death game. To pay for the trip, the Montreal club promised the Rivulettes part of the gate receipts. Preston businesses donated $75 and the town council of Preston donated $25 towards the trip.

Gate Receipts

Gate receipts are the amount of money collected through ticket sales for a sports event. In women's hockey, visiting teams were usually offered a percentage of the gate receipts to help pay their travel costs.

On Friday, March 23, eight players and Coach Fach boarded an afternoon train heading east. The team was buzzing with excitement. If they beat the Montreal Maroons they'd get another chance at the national title.

The game was played at the Montreal Forum — home of the National Hockey League's Montreal Canadiens — in front of over 1,000 fans. The Rivulettes stepped onto the ice on Saturday evening and showed that they were the faster skaters and better stickhandlers. The first goal was scored 11 minutes into the first period when Myrtle Parr and Gladys Hawkins broke from the Preston blue line and raced toward Montreal's end. Gladys slid the puck across to Myrtle, who drove it into the corner of the net. Five minutes later, Helen Schmuck brought the fans to their feet. She went the length of the ice on her own, rushing through the defence and rifling the puck into the net. Nine minutes into the second period, Helen scored her second goal of the game, giving the Rivulettes a 3–0 lead.

Three minutes later, Montreal forward Gladys Kendrick slapped in a rebound in an effort to get Montreal back into the fight. In the last period, Helen banged home her third goal of the game to secure the Rivulettes a 4–1 victory over the Montreal Maroons. The newspaper reported that "the front line of Helen Schmuck, Hilda Ranscombe and Marm Schmuck played brilliantly, backchecking excellently

The Preston Rivulettes in 1934

and keeping the Montrealers well away from Nellie Ranscombe's net." The stick-handling ability of Hilda Ranscombe awed the fans. Before the game was over they gave her the nickname "Joliat" Ranscombe after NHL player Aurèle Joliat, star of the Montreal Canadiens.

The Rivulettes were Eastern Canadian Champs and they had earned a spot in the national finals.

Money in the 1930s

In 1935, the average yearly salary in Canada was $1500. A Ford car cost approximately $500.

It was Preston's turn to host the national final series. Their opponents were the Edmonton Rustlers. It was a chance to take back the title after the defeat in 1933. But the host team always paid the other team's expenses and the Rustlers needed $1500 to make the trip. The Rivulettes tried hard to raise the huge sum of money, but they couldn't do it. It was impossible!

Sadly, the Rivulettes had to hang up their skates. They were forced to forfeit the Canadian title. The Rustlers remained national champs by default. The *Toronto Daily Star* called it a "soft championship," since Edmonton won without having to compete for it.

6 Changing the Rules

The Preston Rivulettes practised hard and by January they were ready for the 1935 hockey season. However, there were problems: bad weather and no teams to play.

The weather was too warm. The Rivulettes had to postpone their first games of the season until later in January when the ice was hard enough to skate on.

The other problem was that there were few women's hockey teams in Ontario to play against. It was the height of the Great

Depression. Teams did not have enough money to travel to play games. People did not have any money to spend on playing sports or the admission price to watch games. More and more teams across the province were folding.

The Rivulettes were able to put a team together, but no neighbouring cities had women's hockey teams. There was no league for them to play in. Toronto had several teams but they were too far from Preston for regular league play.

In the end, the Rivulettes played two exhibition games against the Toronto Pats in January. The Rivulettes were much stronger than the Toronto team. The *Galt Daily Reporter* wrote: "their aggressive plays and their fast moving backchecking efforts baffled the visitors." The Rivulettes easily beat the Pats in both games with scores of 10–0 and 5–1.

Then controversy struck.

Recruiting Imports

The Rivulettes were so good that people thought they were hiring women from bigger cities to play on the team. Recruiting imports was not allowed. But this accusation was completely false. In 1935, all of the players on the Rivulettes were born and raised in Preston, Hespler, or Galt, the three towns where the Rivulettes were allowed to recruit players. Coach Fach told the newspapers and hockey officials that "no girl has ever been imported to Preston and never will be."

On February 1, a telegram from Gus Gaeber, a reporter with the *Montreal Herald*, came to the *Galt Daily Reporter* newspaper office. The letter stated that the Rivulettes were barred from the LOHA playoffs. The Rivulettes and Coach Fach were bewildered and upset by the news. They didn't know why it had happened. The letter did not explain what they had done.

The following day, Coach Fach found out the reason the Rivulettes were being barred from the playoffs: they were not playing in a regular season league. According to the rules, a team had to compete in a league or against at least three teams before they could enter a quarter-final, semifinal, or championship.

In the end, Myrtle Cook, president of the DWAHA, forced the LOHA to change its rule. The Rivulettes could enter the playoffs after playing against just one other team — Toronto. Hilda Ranscombe and her teammates would get another chance at the national title.

The Rivulettes were becoming known as excellent hockey players. Newspapers across Ontario reported their victories.

In March, the Rivulettes played Bracebridge in the Ontario finals. The *Galt Daily Reporter* wrote: "Northern Club gives the locals their toughest opposition of season."

It was a rough game. Four players were given penalties, including Helen Prentiss and Kit Fryer from Bracebridge, and Helen Sault and Helen Schmuck from Preston. The Bracebridge women played the best hockey they could, but they couldn't keep up with the Rivulettes. With Hilda Ranscombe scoring one goal and Marm Schmuck taking care of three more, the Rivulettes easily beat Bracebridge 4–0.

It was their fifth straight Ontario title! They had been playing as a team for five years and no other team in Ontario had beaten them. After the game, Mayor Richards from Bracebridge presented the Rivulettes with the Fanny Rosenfeld Trophy. The Rivulettes were once again on their way to the national finals.

In March of 1935, the Rivulettes met the Montreal Maroons in the Eastern

Canadian semifinals. The Maroons travelled to Ontario for the series. Tickets for the two games were sold at the *Galt Daily Reporter* newspaper office. They were 40 cents each for reserved seats, 25 cents for general admission and 10 cents for children. The Rivulettes hoped to make a profit on the games. They needed the money to travel to Prince Edward Island for the Eastern Canadian finals.

It was an exciting series for the town of Preston. The *Galt Daily Reporter* wrote: "Hockey fandom set a new record attendance for ladies' hockey at the local ice palace last evening, approximately 1,000 paid customers clicking the turnstiles, while 500 school children were guests at the fixture and made their presence known throughout." It was one of the biggest crowds the Rivulettes had ever played for.

It was also the first time that two refs

were used on the ice to keep the game in control — usually there was only one. The refs were busy! There was a lot of body-checking and stick wielding as the teams battled on the ice. The Rivulettes were better skaters and stickhandlers. The *Galt Daily Reporter* declared Hilda Ranscombe "a natural," "a sweet puck-carrier and backchecker," and "the best player on the ice." Playing with new hockey sticks that were a gift from a Preston businessman, the team was led to victory by Marm Schmuck. She scored all three goals, a hat trick, for the Rivulettes for a first game score of 3–1.

The second game was played under poor conditions. It was warm outside and there was an inch of water on the ice. It was hard for players to pass the puck or skate fast. After three frustrating periods, the game ended in a 0–0 draw. Luckily, the combined score meant that

the Rivulettes won the series.

Next up — the Eastern Canadian finals against the Summerside Primrose A.C. team from Prince Edward Island.

The Summerside team guaranteed the Rivulettes $500 to help with their travel expenses. The town council of Preston presented the team with an additional $100. Only seven Rivulettes players, Hilda and Nellie Ranscombe, Helen and Marm Schmuck, Helen Sault, Myrtle Parr, and Gladys Hawkins, made the trip to Prince Edward Island. It was too expensive to send a large squad. But that did not matter for the fast-skating Rivulettes.

After a long train ride and with only a few hours to rest, the Rivulettes stepped onto the ice ready to play. Helen Schmuck started the scoring early in the first period when she picked up the puck and shot it past Dot Harris in the Summerside net. Gladys Hawkins continued in the second period, scoring with a long shot from the blue line. In the third, Marm Schmuck secured the victory with two more goals. The Rivulettes easily beat Summerside 4–0.

It was the first loss for the PEI champions since they organized in 1928. They were not happy about it. They vowed that the second game in the series would not be a blowout. Fans back in Preston waited to hear the results of the game through the local radio station. The Rivulettes had their work cut out for them. The first period was scoreless. In the second, Irene Silliphant drove a hard one into the Rivulettes' net past an astonished Nellie Ranscombe. Twelve minutes into the third, Helen Schmuck evened the count by firing the puck into the Summerside net. After countless attacks by both teams, the final score was 1–1. The Rivulettes defeated the Summerside team 5–1 over the two-game series. They were the Eastern Canadian Champs!

The Rivulettes returned home late in the evening, after 11 p.m., so they didn't think anyone would be there to greet them. They were wrong. A crowd of fans met them at the train station. An unplanned parade took place as six cars piled with fans and players toured the main street of Preston. They tooted their horns. They wanted the whole town to know that the Rivulettes were home and they were champs!

7 Champions of Canada

After winning the Eastern Canadian Championship the Rivulettes were anxious to move on to the national title. They were hoping to play the Edmonton Rustlers to avenge their loss years before. But it wasn't meant to be. The Rustlers played a few exhibition games in 1935, but there was no city league for them. They did not compete for the Alberta or Western Canada title. Like many women's teams in the mid-1930s, they disbanded by the end of the season.

The Winnipeg Eatons were the Western Champions in 1935. It was the Eatons the Rivulettes would have to beat. The Rivulettes were the hosts for the final series. It was the first time the National Championship was played in Ontario. The Rivulettes wanted to win in front of their home crowd.

The Eatons were going to be a tough team for the Rivulettes to beat.

LADIES' HOCKEY

Dominion Semi-Finals

Galt Arena

MONDAY and TUESDAY

April 3 and 4

WINNIPEG
"Olympics"
vs.
PRESTON
"Rivulettes"

Two game series, goals to count on the round.

General Admission 25¢
Reserved Seats 35¢-50¢
Box Seats 75¢

Reserved plan at STAR ELECTRIC STORE, Preston, Phone 453; HIMES' TOBACCO STORE, Galt, Phone 1487, and GALT ARENA, Phone 1300.

The Eatons had been together for two years. They were a rough team with a style of hockey similar to the Rivulettes'. Sammy McCallum coached them. He had played defence for the Winnipeg Falcons when they won the Canadian Junior Championship in 1921.

In the first game of the two-game series, the Rivulettes captured a six-goal lead, with Helen Schmuck scoring four of the goals. Alexandrine Gibb wrote in the *Toronto Daily Star*: "Nearly 2,000 wildly enthusiastic fans witnessed 60 minutes of premier hockey as the rival female pucksters spurred on by the glamour of the occasion and the desire to be the possessors of the Lady Bessborough Trophy, emblematic of the Dominion honours, displayed the greatest exhibition of ladies' hockey ever witnessed in this district."

It was an exciting game with lots of action. The more goals the Rivulettes scored the more frustrated the Eatons players became. Gibb wrote: "Tempers flared, sticks and fists flew in reckless abandon as the rival players dropped the foils, the total of 17 penalties, including two majors, barely being indicative of the rough style of play. Fights took place on and off the ice, with over enthusiastic spectators starting Donnybrooks in various sections of the arena." In the middle of the second period Marm Schmuck dropped her stick at centre ice and exchanged punches with one of the Winnipeg forwards. They had to be pried apart by the refs and they were both given major penalties. The play was rough but it was also fast. The Rivulettes' front line of Helen and Marm Schmuck and Hilda Ranscombe made solo and combination attacks that got them to the net again and again. The final score of the game was 7–1 for the Rivulettes.

Following the game, the players were scolded for their rough style of play by Alexandrine Gibb: "Athletic girls do not often lose their tempers in any game. They have been taught that it is very bad indeed for the boys to do that, but it is practically fatal for girls. Girls can't afford to stage shows of that kind if they want to keep in sport." Many people still did not think women should be playing hockey and certainly not fighting on the ice. But it was clear that this was the type of hockey the fans wanted to see.

After the excitement of the first game, 3,000 spectators flocked to the arena for the second game of the series. It was the largest crowd Preston had seen for hockey in over a decade. People were drawn to the arena to see what all the fuss was about. Fans came from as far away as Montreal with large groups from Toronto, Hamilton, and Guelph. They had to delay the start of the game for 45 minutes so all of the fans could get into the arena!

During the game, tempers flared with lots of tripping and boarding. But there were no fights. The *Galt Daily Reporter* wrote: "Miss Ransom was the pepperpot of the club and every time she stepped out onto the ice fireworks started, especially if Gladys Hawkins of the Rivulettes happened to be on the ice at the same time. They carried on their own private war, and the crowd went for it in a big way."

Both teams were focused on winning. There were no goals in the first period. In the second, Hilda took a pass from Helen Schmuck and drove a high shot towards the Eatons' net. One of the Winnipeg players stuck out a glove to deflect the puck but ended up sending it straight into the net. The score was 2–0 for the Rivulettes. To make up for her teammate's mistake, Yvette Lambert, left-winger for the Eatons, grabbed the puck around the thirteen-minute mark. She skated around the Rivulettes' defence to go in close on Nellie Ranscombe and fire a shot over her left shoulder. In the last period, Gladys Hawkins drove a hard shot into the top corner of the net to give

The Lady Bessborough Trophy

The Lady Bessborough trophy was first given as the prize for the national title in 1935. The Countess of Bessborough, the wife of the Governor General of Canada, donated the trophy.

the Rivulettes a 2–1 lead. The game was clinched when Gladys accepted a puck from Marm Schmuck and rushed the net to score again. The total shots on goal were Preston 31 and Winnipeg 11.

What a game! The Rivulettes had won the Lady Bessborough Trophy. That was the Rivulettes' first taste of widespread fame. They had achieved their dream — for the first time they were the Canadian Champs of women's hockey!

To celebrate the achievement, the town of Preston held a banquet in honour of their team. Sports leaders from across

Canada joined. Those who couldn't be there, like P. J. Mulqueen, President of the Canadian Olympic Committee, sent letters and telegrams of congratulations. Over a hundred people were at the event. The town presented each member of the Rivulettes with an engraved wristwatch. The coaching staff received a silver water pitcher. It was an important moment for the Preston Rivulettes. Accounts honouring the team were found on the pages of the local *Galt Reporter*, the *Toronto Globe* and the *Toronto Daily Star*. The Rivulettes were the best hockey players in Canada.

8 Money Problems

Money, and not enough of it, was a huge problem for women's hockey teams across the country by the mid-1930s. It was the height of the Great Depression. Many people were without jobs and most did not have extra money to spend on playing and watching sports. It was hard for teams to raise the funds to travel. The Rivulettes continued to play fewer games during the season as there were not as many teams in Ontario for them to challenge. The teams they did play, they easily defeated.

In 1936, there were only four teams playing in the western Ontario LOHA league: Preston, the Port Dover Sailorettes, the Toronto Pats, and the Toronto Ladies. A short season of nine games was organized. The schedule got even shorter halfway through the season when the Toronto Ladies dropped out of the league. They did not have the money for gas to travel to Preston and Port Dover for away games. The LOHA decided that there would be no playoffs that year. The club at the top of the standings at the end of the season would be the winner.

On February 20, after a game between the Rivulettes and the Sailorettes, the *Galt Daily Reporter* wrote: "An impromptu and short lived fisticuff display in the dying moments of the game provided further interest for the few adult fans as Eva Smith, visiting defence performer, dumped Hilda

Ranscombe to the ice and then proceeded to pummel the local player who was in no position to retaliate." The players had to be pulled apart by the referee. The Sailorettes hated that they always lost to the Rivulettes. They often got angry on the ice when they were losing. The Port Dover coach was sent a letter from the President of the LOHA, Bobbie Rosenfeld. In the letter, Smith was given a strict warning. She was told that if it happened again, she could be suspended from all women's sports in the province.

At the end of the season, the Rivulettes were the league winners. Next up — the Ontario semifinals against the Stratford Aces. Stratford was a new team. It was the first season they had played together.

The Rivulettes had been playing for six seasons. Most of the players had remained the same and they had a lot of experience. Forward Helen Schmuck had retired after the previous season, but forwards Hilda Ranscombe, Marm Schmuck, and Gladys Pitcher were as strong as ever. They executed attack after attack on the Stratford net. Stratford put up a good fight but the Rivulettes defeated them 4–1 in the first game. There were no surprises in the second game. The Rivulettes won the game 4–0 along with a place in the Ontario finals.

The Rivulettes wanted a sixth Ontario title, this time by playing the Gravenhurst Muskokas. In front of a large crowd at the Gravenhurst arena, the Rivulettes dazzled watchers with their hard shots, careful passes, and perfect plays. In the first period Hilda Ranscombe rushed the net. She gave the Gravenhurst goalie no chance to stop the puck as it sailed past. Three minutes before the period ended, Gladys Hawkins scored with an assist from defence player Helen Sault to make the score 2–0 for the Rivulettes. There were no goals in the second, as both goalies excelled in the net. The third frame brought fans to their feet. Mabel Manson put Gravenhurst on the board with a hard shot to the

Ladies' Ontario Hockey Championship Final
—2nd Game—
GRAVENHURST
Vs.
PRESTON
"Rivulettes"
Preston Arena
Tuesday, March 10
at 8.30 p.m.
Reserved seat plan open at E. J. Mosack's Store at noon on Monday.
Reserved Seats 45c, including tax.
General Admission 30c, including tax.
Children 10c.

top corner of the net. Gladys Hawkins got one back, increasing the lead of the Rivulettes to 3–1. It was close again when Ethel Ronald drove one in for the Gravenhurst team. On a power play, Gladys secured the game for the Rivulettes when she batted a flying puck from the air into the net for a hat trick. The final score was 4–2 for the Rivulettes.

The second game took place in front of a small hometown crowd of 400 people. It was a blowout. The Rivulettes won 5–0. The *Galt Reporter* wrote "With speed, goals, and happy smiles the red jerseyed Preston Rivulettes romped merrily to the top of the LOHA and carved their names on the Fanny Rosenfeld Trophy by an impressive 9–2 victory over Gravenhurst Muskokas." The Rivulettes were clearly the better team. It was their sixth Ontario title in a row.

That year the Eastern Canadian series was in Montreal at the end of March. Before they left for Montreal, the Rivulettes were given a warning from Fred Jackson, a reporter for the *Toronto Daily Star*. He told them that the Maroons had greatly improved from the previous seasons. Although the Rivulettes had never lost to the Montreal team, that year might be different. He told them they needed to be aggressive and fast to win.

But the Maroons proved to be no threat to the Rivulettes. The Rivulettes easily won the series with a 4–0 blowout in the first game and a solid 5–2 win in the second. It was the second Eastern Canadian title for the Rivulettes.

The team from Preston was becoming recognized as the best women's hockey team in Canada. News of their win was even reported in the *New York Times* newspaper. Coverage in the *New York Times* meant that the Rivulettes were known beyond Canada as the best women hockey players in the country.

The Rivulettes' trip to Montreal had cost a lot of money. The Montreal club did not give the Rivulettes help with their expenses. And they didn't advertise the games enough to draw a big crowd to watch the game. The Rivulettes found it eerie playing in the Forum this time. At

A Rule Change

In 1936 the DWAHA changed its regulation that the host team pay the expenses of the visiting team. Having the host team pay was no longer working since none of the teams had very much money.

the first game there were only 526 fans in an arena that could seat over 9,000 people. At the second game there were only 168 people in the stands! Preston's manager Marvin Dykeman was dismayed at the poor turnout. Preston was able to get more fans to a game in their small town than Montreal, a city of over one million people. Women's hockey was clearly not as popular in Quebec as it was in Ontario. The Rivulettes lost a lot of money in their trip to Montreal. They were not sure if they could afford to go to Winnipeg for the national finals.

It was Winnipeg's turn to host the national finals. The Rivulettes were offered half of the gate receipts to help cover the costs of the trip. To travel to Winnipeg they would have to find money for train fare, hotel stays for the three nights they would be there, and their food. After their expensive trip to Montreal, the Rivulettes knew the team couldn't afford it. They presented Winnipeg a counter-offer: half of the gate receipts for the Eatons to come to Preston instead. The Winnipeg team said no.

The Rivulettes coaches tried to raise money to make a better offer. The Preston club was able to offer Winnipeg half the gate receipts and $300 cash if they came to Preston. But, once again, the Winnipeg club said no. They needed more money to make the trip.

So the Rivulettes had a decision to make: pay to travel to Winnipeg or lose

Raising Funds

The Rivulettes' coaches went door to door in Preston asking people for support. There are stories that coach Herb Fach borrowed money against his house to help the team. While businesses and fans gave what they could, it wasn't very much. People didn't have any extra money.

by default. In the end, the Rivulettes had to hang up their skates for the season and default the national title for a second time.

Women's hockey was facing huge money problems. What would the future hold?

9 Fan Support

Few teams and little money again marked the 1937 season. After only a few regular season games, the Rivulettes defeated the Stratford Maids and the team from Markdale in the provincial playoffs to claim their seventh Ontario title.

There was no Eastern Canadian Championship that year. The Montreal Maroons did not have the money to compete. They were forced to default to the Preston Rivulettes.

For once, the Rivulettes' road to the national finals was one with few blocks. It was decided that Preston would host the Western champs, the Winnipeg Olympics, for the series. Bobbie Rosenfeld, president of the LOHA, stepped in to arrange the series on behalf of the Preston team. After bargaining, Winnipeg agreed to accept half of the gate receipts, and to pay for the rest of the trip themselves.

The Winnipeg team of ten players, with two coaches and a chaperone, came by train. They arrived at Union Station in Toronto on Thursday, April 8, the day of the first game. The Winnipeg players were much younger than the Rivulettes, most of them still in their teens. The Rivulettes had five players that had been with the team since the start. Most of the players were now in their early twenties. They had experience and skills, and they were ready to win.

Unlike interest in other women's teams, the Rivulettes' fan following was still strong. In front of 2,000 spectators, the first game of the series opened with the Rivulettes on the attack. Marm and Hilda were the stars of the evening. Hilda ripped two goals and Marm fired one past the goalie for a final score of 3–1. Alexandrine Gibb covered the game, writing that there was "a band, four policemen, a couple of firemen, two capable referees, and a crowded house with a radio broadcast" at the game. Gibb also wrote that this was women's hockey's "debut into big time sport." The Rivulettes were celebrities in Ontario and people flocked to the arena to watch them play.

But something funny happened during the game. Because fans in Preston were used to their team winning all the time, they cheered for the Winnipeg team instead! The Winnipeg team was quite surprised by the cheers they got when they stepped on the ice. The *Galt Reporter* wrote: "the entire arena stood and shouted its delight, when Margaret Topp and Maureen Gault of Winnipeg pushed the puck behind Nellie Ranscombe for their first and only goal of the evening." During a practice after the first game, NHL hockey player Norman Himes visited the Winnipeg team to give them some pointers on beating the Rivulettes. Himes was from Galt, Ontario, and a fan of Preston. But like many people, he wanted to see a closer hockey match. At the second game, there were 3,000 spectators. Despite Himes' advice, the Olympics lost with a score of 4–2.

The Rivulettes were national champs and the rightful owners of the Lady Bessborough Trophy again.

After the series was over, both teams were invited to Maple Leaf Gardens in

Toronto. They were guests of honour at the junior men's hockey final. The Winnipeg Monarchs were competing for the Memorial Trophy against the Copper Cliff Redmen from Sudbury.

The DWAHA were hoping that the men's league, the Canadian Amateur Hockey Association (CAHA) would give them a grant. Bobbie Rosenfeld asked Cecil Duncan, president of the CAHA for help. But, at the end of April in 1937, their request was denied. They would have to figure things out on their own. In September 1937, Myrtle Cook resigned as president of the DWAHA. Bobbie Rosenfeld took over and continued to support and organize women's hockey across the country. She fought to find ways to increase finances and the number of teams playing.

The Preston Rivulettes also had to find more money to keep playing. Before the

Sponsorship

Sponsorship is when businesses provide support to a team (or an event, activity, person, or organization) through money or by providing products (such as new hockey jerseys) or services.

1938 season, this aid arrived in the form of sponsorship by a local business: the Preston Springs Hotel. The hotel helped buy new uniforms and equipment that was badly needed. For the 1938 season, the Rivulettes wore brand new uniforms. Their sweaters were still red and white with a big P on the front, but now "Springs" was written across them. They were called the Preston Springs Rivulettes.

10 New Recruits

At the first practice in 1938, the Rivulettes put out an invitation in the local newspaper. They wanted new players to try out for the team. Some of the older players, like Helen Schmuck, had retired and the Rivulettes needed younger players with lots of energy and skill.

Ruth Dargel played her first game with the Rivulettes' hockey squad on February 5, 1938. Only sixteen years old, she was one of the youngest players on the team.

Ruth Dargel

Ruth started playing hockey when she was a small child. She had four older brothers who let her play with them when they needed extra players. But there was a problem. She only had speed skates. One of her brothers convinced their dad to buy her a pair of proper hockey skates. Ruth's mother got her a place on the Rivulettes hockey team. Herb Fach's son was the Dargels' mailman. When he was delivering mail to their house, Ruth's mom told him that her daughter played hockey and he told her to bring Ruth to the arena to try out for the team.

Ruth was a strong addition to the team. The *Galt Daily Reporter* wrote: "This new player possessing a hard shot and a good turn of speed will strengthen the Rivulettes' attacking division."

To recruit new teams to the area, the Rivulettes and the Stratford Aces held

Ruth Dargel

exhibition games in nearby cities such as Woodstock. They hoped women would form teams and enter the league the following season. They wanted women's hockey to survive.

The exhibitions drew big crowds. More than 1,000 spectators turned out to the Woodstock arena to watch the Rivulettes play the Stratford Aces. Stratford was missing some of their players, so the

Games for Show

Exhibition Games were sometimes played to demo the sport and recruit new teams. The games also helped teams raise money and attention for women's hockey. The results did not count towards the season's total.

Rivulettes loaned them Ruth Dargel. The Rivulettes beat the Aces 8–1. The fans were pleased with the game and it seemed like a women's team would be well supported by the city.

For the 1938 season the Rivulettes formed a league with the Stratford Aces and a new team, the Hamilton Tigers. The Rivulettes went undefeated through the 1938 season. They easily beat the Stratford and Hamilton teams in every league game.

In the Ontario finals the Rivulettes beat the Ottawa Rangers with a 9–2 series score. Several Toronto Maple Leaf players, including Turk Broda, Bill Thorns, Buzz Boll, and George Parsons (who dropped the opening puck), drove down to watch the game. They were impressed by the front line of Hilda Ranscombe, Marm Schmuck, and Gladys Hawkins.

The second game of the series was rough, with lots of stick-swinging and near fights. Eleven penalties were handed out by Referee Maurice Walker — six to Preston and five to Ottawa. The Rangers were no match for the Preston club. The final score was 6–1. The Rivulettes were champs of Ontario for the eighth year in a row.

The Eastern Canadian Championship and the Dominion Championship both took place in Ontario that year. At the beginning of April, the Charlottetown Islanders travelled to Preston to challenge the Rivulettes for the Eastern Canadian Championship. The Rivulettes easily won

Yvonne Richards

Yvonne was one of the oldest women playing hockey in Ontario during the 1930s. She played for the Ottawa Rangers. A mother of five, she was 43 years old. In the 1920s she played with the successful Ottawa Alerts team.

the first game 5–1. During the second game a fist fight broke out between Norma Hipel, a new recruit to the Rivulettes, and Margaret Gallant. Referee Walker separated them before any harm was done and sent them to the penalty box to cool off. Toronto's *Globe and Mail* newspaper reported that the third period of the game was a scramble when "everybody from the goalers out discarded gloves and sticks to really go at it." Thirteen penalties were handed out, eleven of them in the third period. The Islanders fought hard but they were no match for the Rivulettes. The final score was 7–1. The Rivulettes easily won the series and kept their reign as Eastern Canadian Champs.

For the national title, the Winnipeg Olympics travelled to Preston. Much improved from the previous year, the Winnipeg team surprised the Rivulettes. The first game was tied 1–1 after the first period. From then on it was a fight. The Rivulettes were the faster team but they couldn't make it work. The Olympics grimly hung on. The first game ended with a 1–1 tied score.

The Rivulettes were worried that they wouldn't be able to beat the Winnipeg team. The second game was a nail-biter. The first period was scoreless. Finally, a Preston goal came in the second period after the Rivulettes peppered the Winnipeg goal with pucks. In the third period, the Ranscombe-Schmuck-Pitcher line scored

Team Jerseys

Teams were not allowed to have advertising on their sweaters in the national finals. Because the Preston Springs Hotel sponsored the Rivulettes, the word "springs" was on their uniforms, and they couldn't wear them. What would they wear to play? In the end, they borrowed sweaters from a Preston boys' team for the first game. For the second game they wore the yellow and black jerseys of the Stratford Aces.

an important goal, putting them up 2–0. By the end of the game, fog made it difficult to see at the south end of the rink. In the end the Rivulettes won the series 3–1.

The Rivulettes were National Champs again. Alexandrine Gibb wrote that it was the "greatest battle for a Canadian Women's hockey title" that she had ever seen.

But across the country, interest in women's hockey was declining. The

Rivulettes were having trouble drawing large crowds as they had in past years. For some games, less than 200 people were in the stands. Gate receipts were down, giving the team less money to keep playing hockey.

11 Where Are All the Fans?

By the end of the 1938 season it was clear that success was starting to be a problem for the Rivulettes. They were too good!

People no longer flocked to watch them. It was boring for fans to watch a team that they knew would win. This was not good for the Rivulettes. Much of the money they needed to play came from their ticket sales. If they didn't draw large crowds they wouldn't have the money they needed to compete.

It was also starting to be hard to recruit new teams to play. Teams across Ontario didn't want to join the LOHA because they knew the Rivulettes would beat them. Instead of joining a league, many teams were just playing exhibition matches. The LOHA decided that for the 1939 season they would split the senior leagues into A and B groups. Maybe a B group would make it easier for weaker teams to join. They wouldn't have to play the Rivulettes. Preston, Stratford, Hamilton, and Toronto remained in the A group. In the B group were Meaford, Markdale, Collingwood, Hanover, and Thornbury. The winner of the B group would play against the winner of the A group as part of the Ontario title playoffs.

The Rivulettes had another great year in 1939. After beating Hamilton, Stratford, and Toronto during league play, they met the Ottawa Rangers for a rematch in the

The Preston team in 1939

Ontario playoffs. The Preston club easily defeated the Rangers in the finals to win their ninth Ontario title.

All over the province there was less interest in women's hockey. The newspapers were not covering the women's hockey games and playoffs. In past seasons there had been detailed coverage of play-by-play action from the games. In 1938 often only the score and the date of the next game was reported. Spectators could no longer follow their local teams as easily.

The Winnipeg Olympics arrived in Preston on Sunday, April 2, for the national semifinals. They were confident that they could beat the Rivulettes. Except for three players, they were the same team that had played against Preston for two years. The Olympics had picked up a new goalie and two new forwards. News reports wrote that these three players made the team much stronger.

The first game took place on Monday, April 3. Hilda Ranscombe and Ruth Dargel were the stars for the locals. Hilda, with her stickhandling skills, led the forwards on attack after attack. Ruth had her best performance since joining the Rivulettes. Nine minutes into the first period, Hilda and Marm raced down the ice. Marm passed the puck to Hilda, who whacked it into the Olympics' net. Just before the period ended, Gladys was unguarded in front of the net. She grabbed a pass from Marm and Hilda to put the Rivulettes up 2–0. It looked like they were going to win with another wide margin.

The Olympics regrouped. They worked hard to score. Thirty seconds into the second period they did just that. Margaret Lumsden rifled in a shot from the wing past Nellie Ranscombe to make it 2–1. The Olympics outplayed the Rivulettes through the second period. But Ruth Dargel came through with what the newspaper called "the prettiest goal of the night." Picking up a loose puck in the centre zone, she went in fast. She confused the Olympics' defence and drilled the puck past the goalie to regain a two-goal lead.

In the final period, the Olympics held the Rivulettes scoreless. But the Olympics scored only one goal. It wasn't enough. The Rivulettes won the game 3–2. The newspaper stated, "the game was no pink tea affair as members of both teams mixed things up." Seven penalties were handed out — five to the Rivulettes and two to Winnipeg.

In the second game of the series, the Olympics were once again no match for the Rivulettes. Both teams fought hard for victory. There were two injuries during the game. A Winnipeg player crashed into the boards and was carried from the ice. They thought that she had broken her leg, but it turned out to be a badly strained ligament. Hilda Ranscombe was injured when she was hit in the face by a high stick. She lost part of a tooth and needed two stitches on the inside of her mouth.

It was three tense periods but the score remained 0–0. And it stayed that way. Games could end in a tie in women's hockey. The Rivulettes won the series 3–2.

Marm Schmuck on the shoulders of Hilda Ranscombe, Nellie Ranscombe, and Helen Schmuck

For the national finals the Rivulettes travelled to Charlottetown, Prince Edward Island, to defend their title as Canadian champs. For some younger players like Ruth Dargel, it was their first time away from home. Ten players left Preston by train for the seven-day trip down East. They made the last leg of the journey by ferry to the island. Travelling on the S.S. Charlottetown ferry was exciting for the players. There was an ice cutter in front of the boat to cut the thick ice and let the ferry get through. It was a rough ride. When the boat reached the shore, the daughter of the Charlottetown Member of Parliament was there to meet the team. She took them on a tour of the city. They saw the Provincial Parliament Buildings and each team member received a coin as a souvenir of their visit.

The Rivulettes were happy to be in Charlottetown but even more excited to play the national series. The two games were played on Saturday, April 8, and Monday, April 10, at the Charlottetown Forum. The Rivulettes easily beat the eastern team with a final two-game score of 11–3.

Compliments of

Compliments of

E. C. Baker

S. A. McDonald's

Imperial Service Station

SOUVENIR SCORE CARD

DOMINION WOMEN'S

HOCKEY FINALS

For Lady Bessborough Trophy

CHARLOTTETOWN FORUM

SATURDAY and MONDAY
April 8th and 10th

ISLANDERS vs. RIVULETTES

BUNBURY FARM

Besides Holstein Cattle, foxes and mink, Bunbury Farm operates a well equipped

RIDING SCHOOL

where mounts can be hired and instruction is given by Vimy Jones. Wonderful country dirt roads, farm roads and woodland trails for riding, jumping, and hurdling instructions.

J. WALTER JONES   TELEPHONE 486-2

Ruth Dargel's souvenir Game Program for the Rivulettes vs Islanders game in 1939

In 1939, several Canadian women's hockey teams were invited to the United States for ten days of exhibition games. Irene Wall, president of the Quebec branch of the Women's Amateur Athletic Federation was asked to name two women's hockey teams for the tour.

When the Rivulettes heard of the invitation, they assumed they would be chosen. They were the best women's hockey team in the country.

But their success worked against them. Teams from Toronto and Montreal were asked to represent Canada.

The Rivulettes were upset. Why were they not invited? Was it because they were too good? Fred Jackson, a reporter for the *Toronto Daily Star* agreed that the Rivulettes were a threat to the "larger centres" of Toronto and Montreal. He felt the Preston team was being treated with "discourtesy and disregard." In his

Barnstorming

The term barnstorming refers to travelling to provide entertainment. The most popular form of barnstorming in the 1920s was stunt flying. Baseball and hockey teams also barnstormed to increase interest in the sport, gain support, and raise money.

column "Spinning the Sports Wheels," he wrote: "Here we have what is easily the outstanding ladies' hockey team in the Dominion over a period of years and they are pushed around for rival puckettes who can't hold a candle or push a puck in the same arena. It seems to me that the promoters in the United States arenas have been badly misinformed in the ladies' hockey around here . . . It is said that the reason the Rivulettes were not invited was that they were so superior to the other girls' teams that the exhibition would be turned into a farce or a three-act comedy."

Alexandrine Gibb thought that the choice of an Ontario team that wasn't the best was to get even with Preston for always beating Montreal so easily. Maybe they wanted a team that was closer to Montreal's skill level to play matches across the country.

It was the opposite of the early days of trying to prove themselves. The Rivulettes now were too good a team. They were being excluded!

12 The End of an Era

Canada entered World War II in September 1939. It was the end of the Depression but the beginning of something even more consuming — the war effort. All resources went to sending troops off to war and supporting those who were fighting. More women entered the workforce to fill jobs left empty by men who joined the army. There was little time left for hockey at the local arena.

The Preston Rivulettes in 1940

For the 1940 season, the Toronto Ladies was the only Ontario team for the Rivulettes to play. The Rivulettes opened their season in mid-January. They easily defeated the Toronto team 2–0 and 6–0 in the first two games. By the end of February, the Rivulettes had won their tenth Ontario title. They beat the Toronto Ladies in every game they played throughout the season. But few fans had the time or money to watch the games.

The Rivulettes were forced to hang

up their skates after only a handful of games. There was no money for teams to travel. Neither the Eastern Canadian Championship nor the National playoffs took place that year.

Women's hockey across Canada was in bad shape by the end of the 1940 season. In Ontario, one of the reasons was the success of the Rivulettes. In ten years of play, the Rivulettes had never lost a game to an Ontario team. As time went on, they got less interest and support from their fans and the town of Preston. Alexandrine Gibb wrote: "It's tough to be a championship team and have people stay away from seeing you play just because you are tops."

The years of the Great Depression had taken its toll. Teams found it difficult to raise money for travel and expenses. Coach Fach told the *Galt Reporter* newspaper, "taking a hockey team across Canada

Back to the Ice or Back to the Kitchen

Men's hockey declined across Canada as well during this time. But after the war, most men's hockey leagues started again. Boys and men playing hockey were able to pick up where they left off. This was not the case for women's hockey. Following the war, women were expected to be in the home, not on the ice playing hockey.

in the height of the Depression was an undertaking fraught with all kinds of problems, money being the main difficulty."

Canada's entrance to World War II marked the end of an era and the death of women's hockey. By the fall of 1941 the Rivulettes had disbanded and newspapers reported that the LOHA had "closed shop." The LOHA was taken over by

Starting from Scratch

Girls and women played exhibition hockey matches in Ontario and across the country through the 1940s and 1950s. But there were no leagues or tournaments until the 1960s. It was not until 1975 that Ontario had a body to organize women's hockey. Since 1975, the Ontario Women's Hockey Association has increased the number of girls and women playing hockey and has run leagues and championships.

the Ontario branch of the Women's Amateur Athletic Federation (WAAF). Roxy Atkins, who was the president of both the LOHA and the WAAF thought that this was the only way to keep both going. But women's hockey still was on its way out. Throughout the 1940s, there were exhibition matches but no organized leagues and no provincial or national finals.

The Rivulettes didn't realize that this was the end. They assumed they'd be back in competition after the 1940 season. But their time was over. They played exhibition games in 1941 and 1942. But by the end of 1942 the team disbanded and all of the players retired.

Hilda and her teammates had achieved their goal. They started a team against all odds. They practised hard and became the best. They made their dreams come true.

They were national champs. The Rivulettes were the greatest women's hockey team in Canada.

Epilogue

Long after the Rivulettes retired in the early 1940s, they were still known as a great women's hockey team. On May 2, 1998, the team was inducted into the Cambridge Sports Hall of Fame. Hilda Ranscombe, Gladys (Hawkins) Pitcher, and Ruth (Dargel) Collins were at the induction ceremony. They celebrated their success as a team with friends, family, and people who supported them over the years. During the ceremony they looked at pictures of the team. They shared stories from the locker room and the ice. They talked about their favourite memories of playing hockey together. They were stars once again.

The success of the Preston Rivulettes is amazing. During their ten years of play no other team in Ontario ever beat them. They won ten Ontario titles and they were national champs four times.

Hilda Ranscombe was the captain of the team and the star player. Complete records of goals scored were not kept, but news reports show her as the top scorer on the team and probably in Ontario. Ruth Dargel remembers Hilda giving her important advice. She stated, "Hilda took me under her wing, showing me some of the finer skills and how to be a professional both on and off the ice. She was our captain and patiently and enthusiastically shared her knowledge and love for the sport." Hilda wanted everyone to be as good as she was and to love hockey as much as she did.

In 1999, Hilda's name and a nomination package was sent to the Hockey Hall of Fame in Toronto. The details included glowing comments about how amazing Hilda was on the ice. Carl Liscombe, a player for the Detroit Red Wings from 1937 until 1946, grew up with Hilda and her sister Nellie. He had played hockey with them on the Grand River. When the kids had picked teams back in Preston, Hilda was always the first one chosen. Liscombe felt that "Hilda was just as good as any boy, and better than most, myself included." Mary McGuire had played for the Stratford Aces. She felt that Hilda was the best female hockey player in the world. In 2001, the *Cambridge Times* called Hilda "Preston's own female version of Wayne Gretzky."

But the 1999 attempt to have Hilda inducted into the Hall of Fame was not successful.

For more than 60 years, no women were inducted into the Hockey Hall of Fame. But starting in 2010, male and female players were considered separately for induction. A maximum of two women are now inducted each year. In June 2010, the Hockey Hall of Fame's selection committee named Angela James from Canada and Cammi Granato from the United States. They were the first two women to be honoured members of the Hockey Hall of Fame.

Many articles, websites, and books state that the Rivulettes were named to the Hockey Hall of Fame in 1963. This is not true. In 1963, the Hall of Fame told Hilda that they wanted to recognize the team by putting their trophy and pictures on display at the Hall's museum. The team members were happy to agree. But it was recognition in the Hall's Museum not an induction into the Hall of Fame.

The Preston Rivulettes are the most successful women's hockey team in Canada. They will always be remembered for their fast skating and sharp shooting. The Preston Rivulettes are hockey legends.

Glossary

Barnstorming: To travel around an area for the purpose of playing in exhibition sports events.

Bodychecking: Using one's body to knock an opponent to the ice or against the boards.

CAHA: Canadian Amateur Hockey Association.

Defence: The players who defend the net and try to keep the other team from scoring.

Donnybrook: An uproar or a free-for-all fight.

DWAHA: Dominion Women's Amateur Hockey Association. Created in 1933, this body organized the national finals.

Exhibition game: A game played to demonstrate the sport to the public.

The game does not count towards the season's standings.

Fanny Rosenfeld Trophy: The top prize for the Ontario provincial champions. Fanny "Bobbie" Rosenfeld from Toronto donated the trophy.

Forward: An offensive player that carries the puck to the other team's net and tries to score.

Government House: The name of the official residence of the Governor General of Canada.

Hat trick: In hockey, this is when a player scores three goals in a single game.

Lady Bessborough Trophy: The top prize for the Canadian Women's Hockey National Championship.

LOHA: Ladies Ontario Hockey Association.

Member of Parliament: An individual elected to the House of Commons as a representative of the voters.

Penalty: When a player is removed from play for breaking a rule on the ice.

Playoff: Games played for a championship.

Power play: A situation where one team has a greater number of players on the ice because a player from the opposing team has been penalized and has to sit out of the game for a period of time.

Tryout: When athletes compete against each other for a spot on a team.

About the Author

Carly Adams is a sport historian at the University of Lethbridge in Alberta. She loves research that lets her talk to people about their sport involvement in the past and ask them about how they remember their experiences. She has published several book chapters, most recently in *Coast to Coast: Hockey in Canada to the Second World War*, and research articles in the *Journal of Sport History*, *Sport History Review*, *Sport in Society*, *Ontario History*, and the *International Journal of Sport Management and Marketing*. Her current projects explore the history of sport in Lethbridge and women's hockey in Alberta during the 1920s and 1930s. She lives in Lethbridge with her husband Jay, son Quinn, and their dog Rosco.

Photo Credits

We gratefully acknowledge the following sources for permission to reproduce the images within this book:

The City of Cambridge Archives: cover (top), p. 14, p. 35, p. 50, p. 55, p. 103, p. 114

The Provincial Archives of Alberta: p. 47

Ruth (Dargel) Collins: cover, p. 15, p. 17, p. 94, p. 109

City of Toronto Archives: p. 107

The Prestonian: p. 29

The Galt Daily Reporter: p. 64, p. 69, p. 80

Index

More gripping underdog tales of sheer determination and talent!

○ RECORDBOOKS

Recordbooks are action-packed true stories of Canadian athletes who have changed the face of sport. Check out these titles available at bookstores or your local library, or order them online at www.lorimer.ca.